ANTHOLOGY OF POETRY
BY
YOUNG AMERICANS®

1995 EDITION
VOLUME XXXIII

Published by Anthology of Poetry, Inc.

©*Anthology of Poetry by Young Americans*®
1995 Edition
Volume XXXIII
All Rights Reserved©

Printed in the United States of America

To submit poems for consideration in the 1995
edition of the *Anthology of Poetry by Young
Americans*®, send to:
> Anthology of Poetry
> PO Box 698
> Asheboro, NC 27204-0698

Authors responsible for originality of poems
submitted.

The Anthology of Poetry, Inc.
148 Sunset Avenue
Asheboro, NC   27203

ISBN: 1-883931-03-7

Anthology of Poetry by Young Americans® is a
registered trademark of Anthology of Poetry, Inc.

The sixth edition of the <u>Anthology of Poetry by Young Americans</u>® has proved to be as exciting and as diverse as our past editions. All subjects are represented. The poets have given us a look at their world. It's full of monsters, best friends, strange adults, snowflakes, dinosaurs, the big game, the first rumblings of romance and concern about the world they will inherit. Only poetry could contain the explosive energy of a child's mind. The poetry of this edition demonstrates that poetry is the best medium for young writers to express themselves. We are convinced that children live and think in poetic images. We tried to present the poems as the author wrote them, in their format and punctuation. We had a wonderful time editing the 1995 edition of the <u>Anthology of Poetry by Young Americans</u>.® We would like to extend a special thanks to all the poets who participated. We are expecting great things from them in the future.

The Editors

A
minute
drop of
moisture
descending
from above.
Reaching its
destination by
rapidity and per-
sistence. Showing
signs of briskness, to
cool tepid air. It crept
from the clouds with languor,
casting dampness throughout
the sky. Not exterminating the sun's
luminary rays.   In some instances it
approaches, promoting darkness and
gray. No matter how dimmed the light
streams become, the refreshment and
exhilaration, still motivates most
souls. The rain will always be..
significant here.

Robyn Hagadorn
Age: 17

SOFTIE

Waving at me from the line,
I feel her comfort
wash over me
as I walk to school.
Consoling me
when no one else is there.
Her open mind
free from judgment.
Returning home,
she still awaits,
warmed from the sun,
eager to soothe.
Absorbing my tears,
my friend,
always here
to chase away the nightmares.
Soft and silky,
faded from the years.
My softie,
blankets me with love.

Katie Shanley
Age: 14

THE EARTH

The earth is a beautiful place,
You can see that on anyone's face.
Who recycled.

If you recycle,
You can have a nicer ride on your bicycle,
You can recycle your cans,
And put on sunscreen before you get a tan.

If you do these things you're helping
yourself and the earth,
And helping a baby to have a healthier birth.

                                        Sarah Medrek

MANTA RAYS

In the days dark depths of the great blue sea,
There lives a creature, with great massive
wings,
With its curious eyes it guards a pearl,
This pearl that shines is the jewel of the sea.

This creature that's black is sleek as a bat,
They say this creature can glide through the air,
Leaping from the water it soars so free.

                                Breton James Brill-Smith
                                            Age: 12

MY LIFE

I accepted Jesus when I was two
Jesus came into my heart and told me
    what to do
I am not to steal
Even if I don't have a nice meal
I should not be bad
For that makes God very sad

When I turned three
I thought not of me
I thought of others
Of sisters and fathers and mothers
    and brothers

When I was four
There was a knock at the door
I was being bad
and I made God sad

When I was five
I was glad to be alive
By then I was very nice
I was not even scared of mice

When I was six
I had a mix
Of laughter and joy
And of knowing God is not a toy

When I was seven
I thought of when I would be eleven
Would that be my time for Heaven?

When I was eight
I could not wait
To tell of Jesus before it was too late

When I was nine
I knew I would shine
To people who worked in a gold mine

Now I am ten
And here I must end.

Tawnya L. Yeager
Age: 10

WILD FLOWERS

Flowers have secrets all their own,
The answers to no one man are known.
To life itself, through aid of sun;
and thus a sequence has begun.
Which ranges from insensate clod
through man's unconscious thoughts to God.
Of secrets of the wind and pine,
of pungent leaf and reaching vine?
Surely the answer is in your power,
since you yourself are such a flower!

Courtney Schweiger
Age: 12

RACISM

People, places, different races.
Fights and killing, no ones willing,
To stop the crying, stop the dying.
Peoples fear by day and night,
is all caused by our eyesight.
All we see is shape and face, not inside,
the important place.
Just slanted eyes, black skin, girls, guys.
We should not care, it isn't fair.
It isn't right,
to make this silly thing a fight.

Josie Slayton
Age: 12

GRASS.

Grass as green, as green as can be.
Green in spring, summer, and fall.
Hibernating in winter.
March, April, May, June, and July.
August, September, and October
Is when green grass is alive.
Grass as beautiful as a fresh red rose.
When the sun rises in the East,
The grass shines so beautiful.

Jason R. Leonovich
Age: 11

I EXALT THE NAME OF THE LORD

I exalt the name of the Lord.
When I want to rob,
I exalt the name of the Lord.
I try to exalt the name of the Lord
When I am angry.
Even when I am not happy,
I still try to exalt the name of the Lord.
I may try to lie or swear and think the Lord
Does not care, but he does.
So I pray and ask his forgiveness and--
I exalt the name of the Lord.

Andy Bennett
Age: 17

JOY

I feel a sense of joy
Whenever I get a brand new toy.
I feel a sense of gladness
When I'm not in sadness.
I feel real happy
When I'm with my pappy.
I feel real pleased
When I'm at ease.

Cletus Christopher Paul Stell
Age: 11

THE COUNTRY

The trees, the crows,
A river that flows;
All in the Country.

Flowers that grew,
An evergreen too;
All in the Country.

There are bees,
But plenty of trees;
All in the Country.

No pollution,
It's mainly evolution;
All in the Country.

See the paths,
But there isn't any wrath;
All in the Country.

Plenty of fields,
Nothing is sealed;
All in the Country.

You can find your rights,
Without any fights;
All in the Country.

Do what you wanted,
Without getting taunted;
All in the Country.

People are kind,
You have a peaceful mind;
All in the Country.

It's all in the country!

Christopher Drost
Age: 9

WHOM DO WE LIVE TO PLEASE?

Whom do we live to please? Whom?
For some, it is their family,
For others, their friends.
Either way, they're always trying to live up
To someone else's expectations,
Sometimes succeeding, sometimes failing.

Whom do we live to please? Whom?
Some spare not a thought for how others
May view their actions.
And there are still others
Who strive only to please God.
These, more often than not,
Find themselves alone
With either their opinions
Or their God.
Whom do we live to please? Whom?

Erin Mitchell
Age: 15

As the forest sleeps
it is quiet throughout night
only one bird sings.

Cindy VanEtten
Age: 11

MY LOST LOVE

I can't stop feeling this way
Every night, every day
I always feel the same
But I will never know that special name.

Michelle Hall
Age: 11

I LIKE

I like to run and play in both my yards,
I like to sit sometimes and play cards.
I like to lay on my bed and read a book,
I like to sit around and just look.
I like to relax and watch TV.
I like to lie back and watch a movie.
Mostly I like to do as I please,
And I like looking and talking in the breeze.

Elizabeth Fox
Age: 11

JUST A LITTLE BABY

It was just a little baby;
So tiny, and yet, so sweet.
You probably feel guilty but that's okay
He lives with angels now on Heaven Street.

It was just a little baby;
You had to make him suffer because
You thought he was a mistake,
But little did you know that during the
procedure,
You put your own life at stake.

It was just a little baby;
You took his life away and
That's a mystery to me.
You could've put him up for adoption,
But that's not how you wanted it to be.

It was just a little baby;
It had no idea what was going on.
Why did you ever have to do that?
It's too late now; the baby's gone.

Stephanie Lockhart
Age: 17

MY SECRET PLACE

Sometimes I take a ride
to a secret place that only I own.
It is my hide-away, my soul's church,
my one true home.

No one follows me there;
a secret place I dare not share.
Mine to hold and grasp tight -
Mine to visit in the endless night.
No one dares disturb my secret place
for it's hidden here behind my face,
with rivers of laughter and hilltops of joy,
using my eyes as the seeing toy.

I use this place to disappear
from the cruelties of a world I long to hate,
where one's hatred of another is solved by a gun,
and the hands of someone else decide one's fate.

My secret place, my dire escape,
guarded by imaginary yellow tape;
my secret place for no one to find,
just me and my secluded mind.

Marina Sabatini
Age: 16

HALLOWEEN

Happy, Happy Halloween,
It's the greatest holiday ever seen,
It's when ghouls and ghosts from everywhere,
Come to make a great big scare,
It's when pumpkins have a scary face,
You'll find them at every place,
It's when skeletons rattle their bones,
They're everywhere, even in your home,
It's when monsters, big and blue,
They'll scare you so, you'll jump out of your shoes,
Happy Halloween is a good song to your ear,
It's sad Halloween only comes once a year.

Krystal Gula
Age: 10

I WENT FISHING

I went fishing
I caught a big fat fish
Then I took it home
And slapped it on a dish
Sizzle! Sizzle! Fry! Fry!
Don't forget
Take out its eye.

Jacob M. Antes
Age: 9

THE TRAIL

One kick,
nothing.

Two kicks,
almost.

Third kick,
engine roars.

First gear,
front wheel off the ground.

Second gear,
loudly screams down the trail.

Third gear,
wind wisps through helmet.

Fourth gear,
front end gets lighter.

Fifth gear,
flying through the trail.

Duane Smith
Age: 15

HALLOWEEN PARTY

Halloween parties are awesomely cool.
It beats watching TV and even shooting pool.
Bobbing for apples is a narley game.
Playing Checkers and Twister is just not the
same.
I love the party punch, its moist and sweet.
Having one cup is a perfectly fine treat.
Halloween parties are so much fun.
The worst part about them is when they're all
done.

Matthew John Karczewski
Age: 11

CHANGING LEAVES

The leaves are changing everywhere.
The leaves are flying through the air.
Pretty colors.
I will see as I walk by the leaves.
Red, yellow, gold and green are the colors of
the leaves.
I pick all the pretty ones and put them my hat,
And when I go home
I show them to my mom, dad and cat.

Jenna Anderson
Age: 10

FALL

Fall, fall
Is the best time of all,
Critters will crawl,
The leaves will fall.
So have a ball,
Then rake them all,
It's fall, fall, fall.

Leaves, leaves
Will blow around,
Then suddenly,
Fall to the ground.
Then have more fun,
Because it will soon be done.

Rachel Marie Livingston
Age: 10

SPRING

Spring, spring is so cool
It's so cool it rules the school.
Once the spring starts to come
School gets much more fun
When school is over it's time to go.
But wait, here we go.

Adrienne Franchi
Age: 10

THE FOUR SEASONS

The sun is shining,
Oh, so round,
No more snow on the ground.
What could this wonderful season be?
It's summer! It's summer!
So much to see!

The leaves are falling off of every tree,
So much to do,
So much to see.
Now the trees are bare,
It's fall, it's fall,
With love and with care!

Snow is falling everywhere,
The ground is white from here to there,
Cold and chill in the air,
The wind is blowing too!
It's winter, it's winter,
A very fun time,
Just for you!

The birds can fly,
See the blue sky.
The flowers are growing,
The wind is blowing.
The children fly kites,
It's spring, it's spring,
See the beautiful sights!

Leanne Trevelline
Age: 10

THE SUN

A ball of yellow light
that goes out when it's night,
but will never go away
because it comes back in the day.

A big yellow star
that is ever so far.
It rises in the east
over a large green beast,
but it sets in the west
so it can take a small rest.

Katie Fairley
Age: 11

FLOWERS

Flowers growing everywhere
Flowers growing here and there.
Have some fun, pick a ton
put them in your hair.
Go down to the mill or
right down the hill and run
through them with glee.
Go down and pick some
just for you and me!

Missy Wichryk
Age: 10

WHAT AM I?

I am little and round,
I bounce on the ground.

I am put in a hoop,
and played with a group.

I am used in a game,
can you guess my name?

It's your call,
yep, I'm a basketball!

Ashley Lokey
Age: 11

THE WINNING SHOT

The score is tied
five seconds to go.
I look over my shoulder
to see where to go.
They give me the pass
I make a three.
We won the game
because of me.

David Izzo
Age: 11

SWANS

This is Dawn
who is a swan.
She has a friend
whose name is Shawn.
Shawn and Dawn
go out on the lawn
they chase each other
and never yawn.
Shawn and Dawn
meet Ron and John.
They fly away
and now they're gone.

Alaina Fairley
Age: 9

EAGLES

Eagles how soft you fly
gliding through the sky.
Your eyes are as sharp as knives,
And claws like steel.
How swift you fly,
In the blue sky.
You see a hundred miles away
into the sky.

Paul Ceriani
Age: 9

Bunnies, bunnies are so sweet.
Bunnies, bunnies can't be beat.
They jump and twitch on your lap.
Their feet always make a tap.

Dayna Mulig
Age: 10

PARROT

I want a parrot
that looks like a carrot.
Smart as a whip,
with a little hip.

Heather Lechner
Age: 10

MY CAT

I have a cat her name is Puddy.
She likes to hunt and bring me goodies.
Field mice, ground squirrels,
Anything that runs.
She chases, and to her it's fun.

Rachel Kost
Age: 11

OUT TO SEA

As I sit upon this rock
Staring deeply at the dock
Watching ships going in and out
Wondering just where, oh where
They're about to go.

About to go and from where they come
O how I'd like to be
Upon a ship going out to sea.
To see the world around the sea
O I hope someday to be
Upon a ship going out to sea.

Michael Yoho
Age: 14

THE BEACH

Ocean waves and sandy shore
   that is what I adore.
Peaceful, quiet, relaxing in the sun
   that sounds like fun.
Sand in your toes and sunscreen on your nose
   be careful not to go into a doze
   or your skin will turn red as a rose.
The sun goes down and everyone frowns
   because another day at the beach is done.

Lisa McConahy
Age: 13

Race car
Expensive, fiberglass
Race, squeal, zoom
Fast ride
Streak of lightning

Brady Baker
Age: 9

Spring
Nice, warm
Dancing, singing, planting, playing
Leaves begin to grow on trees
Swimming, biking, batting, sleeping
Hot, humid
Summer

Matthew Yowonske
Age: 8

Summer
Hot, swimming
Running, jumping, fun
Summer has a lot of fun things to do.
Sweaty, nice, fishing, exciting
Raining, hot, fun, swimming, nice
Fall

Monica Sloan
Age: 8

There once was a boy named Rick.
Who sat on a roof and threw a brick.
His last name was McNeil.
He had a pet seal.
That he took to an afternoon flick.

Thomas McNeil

SCHOOL

School
Fun, Cool
Learning, Playing, Writing
Nice Place
Cool Adventure

Katie Crawford
Age: 8

Winter
White, deep
Snowing, frosted, clouded, raining
There is a white glow all around.
Growing, brightening, shining, planting
Hot, humid
Spring

Eliot E. Schmidt
Age: 9

GHOSTLY, GRIM, AND GRUESOME

Ghosts come out on Halloween!
They'll keep haunting you until you scream!
If you don't, they'll shoot you with a beam!
That will melt you into hot, hot steam!

Keith Volk
Age: 8

HALLOWEEN NIGHT

Ghosts fly high on Halloween night.
They'll give you a big fright.
On Halloween night the moon is bright.
The witches are filled with total delight.

Caitlyn Sauritch
Age: 9

Summer
Fun, hot
Jumping, swimming, running, kicking
Summer is very hot.
Chilling, running, blowing, falling
Joyful, colorful
Fall

Amber Godfrey
Age: 8

WHO YOU ARE IS GOOD

My mom said,
if you try hard and you practice enough
you'll get good at something.
But I practice hard and I try hard
and it doesn't work.
I want to be the best speller in the world
but it will never be possible.
I want to win an award for my math
but it will never be possible.
I want to read out nice and clear
and have everybody understand it
I want to know every state capital
and have everybody think I am smart
but it will never be possible.
I want my handwriting to be perfect
but it will never be possible.
But I know that nobody is perfect
and I am proud of myself
for what I can do

Abigail Blum
Age: 8

THE PERFECT BUFFET

Mounds and mounds of food
What do I pick
Waffles with thick blueberry syrup
And heaps of whipped cream
Danish filled with jelly and swirled with icing
Shiny, golden brown croissants
Two of these...
Yes that sounds really good
Now for the last thing
Warm oatmeal with brown sugar
In my mouth...delicious!

Althea Jenkins Webber
Age: 8

THE RAINBOW

Now that the storm has o'er us passed
And the rain ceased upon the earth --
Clouds have parted and flown away.
So softly and humbly it fills the sky
Sought by the patient eye.
A faint line of promise,
A token of a sacred oath
Has faded away.

Heidi Gerlach
Age: 16

BEAUTIFUL KITE

Flying free, flying high,
Beautiful kite up in the sky.

Your colorful tail floating by,
Beautiful kite up in the sky.

Twisting, twirling, you catch my eye,
Beautiful kite up in the sky.

Flying free, flying high,
Beautiful kite up in the sky.

Erin Brown
Age: 11

FALL

It's the end of fall
sometimes it snows
sometimes at night, I hold my doll tight
at night, I turn on my light in the night
now I can't fly my kite
soon Jack Frost will bite.
Jack Frost and I will fight,
and I'll punch him in the nose
and then he will fall.

Jessica Wille
Age: 6

Your eyes open slowly as you get up from the floor.
A blue coldness erupts from inside your decaying core.

You stumble across the room as the ceiling draws away.
The voice in your head screams,
But no one hears what it tries to say.

The walls envelope you and the rainbow of
Flying colors drip from the sky.
You collapse from the cold and the pain
Wants to make you die.

Dazed, the walls hurl you through the golden gates
Into the black space.
The dim glowing sun fades away and the calm moon
Is there to replace.

The deep darkness overwhelms you and the
Black holes enchant your eyes to close.
Breathing air of the stars, looking through time,
Sights unseen to man are at your dispose.

A tremor moves you when the mass of question
And sun smashes.
Suddenly you're awake,
And another celestial daydream passes.

Ed Vargo
Age: 13

BASKETBALL FOREVER

I got warmed up,
I laced up my shoes.
The whole visiting crowd is against me,
As they let out their Boo's.

It seems like everyone is against me,
That there is nobody that is left.
They're all trying to distract me,
Even the Ref.

My team shoots some shots,
To warm up the crowd.
The visitors hate us,
They're expressing it loud.

The warning buzzer sounds,
That's the start of the game.
The whole crowd is there,
It's all just the same.

The jump ball flies up,
It just floats in the air.
Then, it started to come down,
We just took it from there.

And right after that,
We just dazzled this team.
Up and down the court,
Like they've never seen.

But somehow, just somehow,
They just started to regain,

Their strength and their talents,
We were losing this game.

Then it came down to it,
The final 1:03.
Our coach brought us into a huddle,
And pointed to me.

You're the man, Tony,
Just get the ball.
Advance, you do that,
Then there is nothing at all.

As the long seconds,
Of the time-out were up,
We all gathered round,
To gain some more luck.

We did our school,
St. E's fighting theme.
1, 2, 3, Lancers!
We shouted as a team.

The 1:03 remaining,
Went slow, and at last,
We reacted to our plan,
So smooth and so fast.

I got the rock,
I went to the hoop.
They couldn't even touch me,
As I said the word Swoop!

I went right around them,
And juggled the ball.
They tried to block it,
But failed in all awe.

The ball left my fingers,
And flew through the air.
It was all up to me,
I could tell it was there.

As the ball hit the hoop,
It bounced all around,
And fell through the net,
Making a loud, swishing sound.

The game was over,
I had won my team the game.
I was the hero,
I had gained the fame.

But all and all,
That's how the story went.
We had won the State Championship,
And that is the end.

Tony DeCosmo
Age: 13

DEAR HOUSE

I wish I had to offer you more than just a
thank you for giving me shelter.
I would make you a card, but you wouldn't
be able to see or read it.
I would give you a present, but you wouldn't
be able to use it.
I would give you a hug, but you wouldn't
be able to hug me back.
I guess all I can do is,
say thank you.

Elizabeth Cuniak
Age: 11

HALLOWEEN

On Halloween night, witches fly on brooms.
Black cats scare.
And devils curse.
Goblins hide in graveyards.
Jack-o'-lanterns grin at you.
The full moon shines over haunted houses.
In October leaves fly like witches on brooms.
Skeletons, bats, and vampires scare.
Ha! ha! ha!

Jessica Davis
Age: 8

WHAT IF HAIR WAS SPAGHETTI

If hair was spaghetti,
Italians would never have to cook,
All they would do,
Is sit around and read a book.

If people wanted to eat,
Spaghetti would be the one,
You could just eat it off your head,
And you would never be done.

For bows or ribbons,
It might look nice,
With pepper, salt, cheese, sauce,
Or a very nice spice.

There is only one bad thing,
Disgusting too.
How would you like to have,
A pot of hair stew.

Helen Karloski
Age: 11

LONG AND EVERLASTING

The sun sets
But it will not rise again.
The wind silently stops
The clouds slowly drift away.
The world becomes a ball of darkness.
In the distance a child is born
So tiny and fragile,
But his soul is so strong.
The father holds the child
As he takes his final breath.
Time stops.
The tears start to pour.
The silent cries
Of the father and mother
Fill the room.
Death has taken another
Small innocent life.
The breath of a child
Long and everlasting...

Leanne KuKuruda
Age: 16

WHY?

Did you ever stop to wonder
why God takes loved ones away?
Whenever their living on,
day to mysterious day.
Thy fragrance surrounds you,
though the spirit is gone, but never forget
in your heart he lives on.
Was it something we did,
or something we said? It's to
late to wonder for now thee is dead.
He ascends to heaven above,
flying through the sky,
like a wondrous eagle,
soaring up so high.
Higher and higher as he disappears,
our love for thee is not forgotten, but
we dry up our tears.
For we know he is going
somewhere loving and sweet,
life can be taken in just one heart beat.
So as we continue on,
take a look into the sky, maybe someday it
will answer our question of why!

Jennifer Costanza
Age: 12

FEELINGS

Roses are red,
The moat is green,
Unicorns are kind,
But dragons are mean.

Jonathan Storrick
Age: 9

WINTER TIME

Winter's coming to be sure,
Knocking hard on Pittsburgh's door.
Bringing with it snow and ice,
Things grown-ups think aren't very nice.
However, when all's said and done,
For kids, winter's a ton of fun.

Marissa Rivers
Age: 9

SOCCER

Soccer is fun when you run.
Sometimes you fall when you have the ball.
Soccer can be fun for anyone!

Brittany Bargerstock

THE LONG WAIT

Santa, Santa, where are you?
The night sky is clear and blue.

I am waiting for you tonight.
I know it will be a great sight!

I'm sure my house
will be as silent as a mouse.

It will be lit up,
as I wait up.

Ashley Leigh Harff
Age: 9

SNAP, CRACKLE AND POP

A roughly-jagged
crunchy sound
made Kara wrinkle her nose.
But when you listen
you can hear
crackling and crumbling sounds.
You think it maybe....
wait a minute, it's just Sarah
eating her Rice Crispies

Heather D'Angelo
Age: 11

NATURAL DISASTER

N ausea
A nger
T umult
U pset
R ain
A ftershocks
L ightning

D anger
I nfuriate
S torm
A wry
S uffering
T urmoil
E ngulf
R ape

Charles A. Burchell, II

STRANGLER FIG

Strangler fig
Green, tall
Beautiful, swaying, trembling
A magnificent living thin
Epiphyte

Jessica Smith
Age: 11

I walk beside millions of trees.
I feel a cool breeze blow through my hair.
I see a squirrel scurry up a tree.
I hear birds whistle little songs.
It is the best time of the year.

Brandon Fowler
Age: 8

I DREAMED I WAS A BEAR

I dreamed
I was a bear
In a river
Eating and playing with other bears
Gratefully.

Adam Trumpie
Age: 11

Summer
Hot, humid
Swimming, biking, swinging, laughing
It begins to grow hotter outside.
Raining, chilling, swaying, dancing
Pretty, colorful
Fall

Shannon Leigh Black
Age: 9

The whole gound is white.
Snow is falling from the sky.
You build a snowman.
You make a bunch of footprints.
Everything is covered in white.

Justin Welsh
Age: 8

F   reedom is the best
R   ochester Rams are no good
E   ven if they win
E   very time we play. Bull
D   ogs are so good, even if they run
O   n the football field, there's a pass
M   y friend, Natalie, is a cheerleader.

Katie Thielman
Age: 8

SPORT

S   ports are cool!
P   ow! The bat hit the ball!
O   h, my, SHAQ slammed!
R   ah! Rah! Cheerleaders cheer
T   ennis Andre Agassi wins the trophy!

Kiel Stroupe
Age: 9

B   ad
R   ough at playing football
U   nited in my family
C   ute when sick, my mom says
E   dward is my middle name.

Y   eager is my last name.
E   nthusiastic I am
A   lot of fun, I am
G   ood kid, sometimes
E   ager
R   egular, not!!!!

Bruce Yeager
Age: 9

TIGERS

Tigers, tigers are so neat
Tigers, tigers can't be beat
They run through the jungle
like prancing deer
And it always feels like
they are near.
They hunt for food
in the trees and weeds.
I sure hope they don't eat me.

Kristina Karczewski
Age: 9

THE DOVE

Together we shall live,
  With happiness and love,
The only thing you'll give,
  Is your graciousness from above.

The love will be returned to you,
  In simple certain ways,
The affection is returned to me,
  For all the rest of my days.

The time is right to give myself,
  The love from God above,
The symbol for this friendship,
  Is the flying dove.

So now you can remember me,
  With those deeply love filled eyes,
For in your heart you soon will notice,
  I've come to live in the skies.

Michelle Maze
Age: 13

THE SKY

The sky is nice and fluffy,
The clouds are really puffy.
They stand out far,
May hide a star,
If you look close you may see a puppy.
Sometimes there might be a bear,
Or maybe even a chair.
There's many more things,
Like four diamond rings.
To see them just look at the air.

Stephanie Plutko
Age: 10

A BLACK AND WHITE LIFE

The homeless wonder the streets,
looking for food and shelter.
Snuggling up under bridges
away from the brisk weather.
Pleading for money, but
especially food.
To me, if their life
was on television it would
be black and white.

Matthew D. Hough
Age: 12

YELLOW

Yellow
Tastes like a
Big milkshake,
The hot yellow
Sun,
Stars that shine
In the sky.
A point of a
Witches hat,
A fan blowing,
A cow mooing,
Rough as a rhinoceros,
A juicy
Lemon,
A fire burning,
Popcorn in the microwave,
A candle that is lit,
Yellow
Leaves are a sign of fall
To come!

Lauren Fritz
Age: 10

WHITE

White looks like a blank paper,
The white Power Ranger,
Or a skeleton.
White smells eerie as glue,
Or nice as a flower,
Or bad as exhaust fumes in the morning.
White tastes like a freshly peeled apple,
The middle of a pineapple,
Or coconut milk.
White sounds like a white Porsche roaring by,
Crunching paper,
Or Dad dropping the truck's hubcap.
White feels like my ceiling,
Gooey as glue,
Or wet as melting vanilla ice cream.

John W. Christ
Age: 9

THE BEAR

Once there was a bear.
He could not go anywhere.
So he ate a solar flare.
The solar flare took him to the fair.
He went on a ride that went nowhere.
It looked like a square.

Anthony Piechnik
Age: 9

THE TORNADO

One morning I woke to a great storm,
And I wished I was never born.

The wind swirled and swirled and blew the
house,
I got frightened at the sight of a mouse.

I was glad when I woke up in bed.
Then I wished I was never dead.

It was only a dream.
I'm so glad, I can scream!

HOORAH!!

Tanya Reynolds
Age: 8

DARE TO DISCOVER

C'mon and discover, I dare you to,
Bring your mother, father, sister, and you.
It's not very hard, it might take some time,
If you want you could quit at quarter to nine.
So, come and discover, I dare you to,
And if you wanna know the truth,
It's not very hard to do.

Jerica Hodgson

MOE THE DOG

In the light of the sun
a little dog run
Away run away way, way, way
how fast or slow little dog Moe will go
Slow or fast he will stay
every second of the day
He will bite your toy bad boys
he will bite your pillow too
Hide them hide
behind you!

Samantha Humanic

A dream is like a noun
A person, place, thing, or idea.
It is my desire, my conquest
The sweepstakes, my Jeep
Cool clothes,
Riches, and fame
To go through the stores
And sign autographs
To own a mall
And have a jet
A dream conquered.

Lolia Adoki
Age: 12

THE LIGHT OF A FRIEND

The sky is gray and hanging down.
The grass has died and all turned brown.
The rain is beating upon the ceiling,
And it knows what I am feeling.
The days are dark and never end.
Then I find the light of a friend.

Danielle Corey
Age: 9

SNOW

Snow is falling all nice and white
children are playing out all night.

When they get sleepy
they come in and take off their mittens,
boots and hats
so they can relax!

They wake up the next morning
go out and see
all the great snow they can play in with me!

When they get cold
they come in and say
Mommy won't you please make us cocoa today.

Justin Guadagni
Age: 8

FRIENDS

A friend is a person...

You like to be around,
When you are sad and blue,
She can pick you right up off the ground.

A friend is a person...

With whom you can share,
Your deepest secrets,
Without getting in your hair.

A friend is a person...

With whom you can act like a clown,
When you act goofy,
She won't tell the whole town.

Our friendship is as solid as stone,
I never have to worry
That I should ever be alone.

Angela Derewonko
Age: 11

THE FORGOTTEN CAKE

My snake baked a cake
He went outside to rake
While the cake was left to bake.
He raked and raked,
Soon he forgot about the cake.
The cake over baked.
The snake dropped the rake
And ran to get the cake,
But it was too late
To save the burnt cake.
What a sad little snake!!!

Benjamin Adams
Age: 9

PLANTS

I like to watch plants grow, grow, grow,
But in the winter no, no, no.
I see the plants grow up straight,
But only on a certain date,
So when spring time comes around,
Plant a seed in the ground,
And when summer is here look and see,
The plant has grown like you and me.

Shelby Zaya
Age: 12

MY DOG AND I

I love animals.
I have a dog named Sissy.
She is a Boston Terrier.
She is small, but long.
Sissy eats, sleeps, even has a tail like a pig.
That's my dog, Sissy.

A.J. Kastriba
Age: 9

GREEN

Green as a golf course,
Bright as money,
Green as grass,
Sounds like leaves falling,
Money being counted,
The grass whistling.
Fells like grass,
paper money,
smooth leaves.
Tastes like a lime,
bad broccoli,
good peas.
Smells like a ripe lime,
fresh grass and
old broccoli.

Zach LaScola
Age: 10

The wind is like a still pond.
The wind feels like water
rushing up against me.
The wind is like a gardener
seeing the first bloom of spring.
The wind helps a kite to sway
back and forth until the dust of dawn.
The wind helps us to feel
good about ourselves,
or just let the problems go by.

In memory of my father, Ed Ryan,
A victim of flight.

Kelly Ryan
Age: 10

WHO DO I TALK TO?

Image in a world where it's safe to play.
To walk on the streets if it's night or day.
Or talk to a stranger and accept candy and treats.
And not to be afraid of what's in your sweets.
I wish we could get rid of guns and drugs.
And pay more attention to kisses and hugs
I know wishes sometimes come true.
So let's all cross our fingers
For tomorrow is me and you.

Valerie Jarmon

HALLOWEEN DAY

On Halloween day I strolled down the hall,
where eerie pictures hung on the wall,

When my footsteps stopped on the floor,
I found myself in front of a door,

Welcome to the fourth grade room,
said a witch with a broom,

From inside 28 eyes shining so bright
ooh, they give me such a fright.

But as I looked inside,
I could tell by their smiles,
this is a place I can stay for awhile.

But there is only one thing to say,
it's so bad being the
new kid on Halloween Day!

Kylie Runtas
Age: 9

A QUARTERBACK

The quarterback says, Go out for a throw!
The running back says, I've nowhere to go.
The quarterback put the ball into the air.
For someone to catch if they would dare.

Daniel Arthur DeDominicis
Age: 9

HALLOWEEN

Halloween what a night,
Such a fright.
You go out trick or treating,
And you get a beating!
For the mummy comes out of his grave,
You try to be brave.
The mummy picks you up,
In his pickup truck!
You get in,
You see a mermaid fin.
He takes you to his house,
You're greeted by his pet mouse!
You SCREAM!
Then you wake up,
And, find out it's a dream.

Jessica Alrutz
Age: 10

FLOWERS

Flowers are cheerful,
Some can be blue.
Fresh ones and sweet ones,
They'll always love you.

They start out as seeds,
Plant them all around.
Water them each day,
And they'll appear from the ground.

Tulips and roses,
All different kinds.
Sometimes I wonder,
If they have their own minds.

They may be oval,
Also they're round.
With jagged petals,
That point to the ground.

Their smell is so lovely,
Like brand new perfume.
The scents from the petals,
All fill up the room.

They're many different colors,
Like red, yellow, and green.
The ones with the needles,
They never act mean.

I love flowers,
I hope you do to.
I already know,
That they sure love you.

Shannon DeMarco
Age: 11

THANKSGIVING

The parades are starting.
The football games are, too.
The turkey's cooking.
All for me and you!

The guests are arriving.
Our celebration has begun.
Everyone's called to the table.
Because the turkey is finally done!

Stephanie Hutchison
Age: 8

Dogs,
Furry, cuddly
Chewing, hopping, barking
A gentle and loving pet
Abby

Johnny DeMarzio
Age: 8

Dog
Careful, playful.
Running, playing, barking.
Quietly sleeping on the bed.
Baby.

Brandi Mannion
Age: 8

Dog
Soft, sightless
Running, walking, hunting
Creeping after a rabbit
Daisy

Sarah Hamilton
Age: 8

THE BUG

There was a bug
On the rug.
I said, go away little bug.
He came up behind me and gave a tug
Please go away little bug.
And the bug said,
I just wanted to give you a hug.

Danielle Steigerwald
Age: 9

TURKEY DAY

Turkey Day is a week away,
Oh, hooray!

Rolls and butter my favorite thing.
I always get the turkey wing.

Pumpkin pie and cranberry Jell-O,
Always makes pappy a happy fellow.

Mom and Heather will set the table.
Grandma will help, if she's able.

We all sit down and give our thanks.
Then we begin to fill our belly tanks.

Shannon Stewart
Age: 9

JUMPING BEAN

David is a jumping bean.
Jump, jump, jump.
Over sister over brother over a big lump.
Over Mommy over Daddy over some toys.
David lands on his knees with a big noise!

Rachel Rorick
Age: 9

strawberries
delicious, luscious
planting, seeding, growing
vine, seed, bushes, bees
tasting, picking, eating
juicy, sweet
raspberries

Jessica Butchki
Age: 10

School
School is fun.
You can't run,
In the hall,
With a ball.
You'll be caught,
And be taught.

Erica Wilson
Age: 8

Cats
Furry, frisky.
Meowing, jumping, playful.
Everyone in my house loves cats.
Tommy.

Kevin J. Miller
Age: 9

RAIN

Rain, rain, falling down,
Falling on our way to town.

Falling, falling, on the ground,
With a gentle tapping sound.

In the store as we go,
Falling gently in a row.

Back outside near the car,
Catching rain in a jar.

Looking up at the sky,
Watching the dark clouds go by.

Falling down in a race,
Dropping on my smiling face.

Now at the car door,
I look at the wet, soggy floor.

Oh no, oh no
Look at the open window!

Now I want the rain to go away,
So I can go out and play.

Susanne Hunt
Age: 12

ENTERING NEW YORK HARBOR

Cold blue waves,
  wash upon the hull.
Overhead, crying for fish,
  swoops a small gray gull.

The sun is slowly rising,
  the sky is turning pink.
Seeing the new day beginning,
  arouses my mind to think.

To the right is Lady Liberty,
  in the dawn her torch gleams.
The rays of light from her crown,
  are freedom's holy beams.

The boat is steadily swaying,
  and the city's skyline is growing.
Around me I feel the warmth,
  the warmth of love overflowing.

As I slowly remember,
  my old hopes and dreams.
Abundant with new ones,
  my elated heart teems.

As I try to forget,
  my old memories and fears.
Down my frost-bitten cheek,
  slips a single tear.

But, now I am in America,
  land of the independent and free.

Who has opened her gates,
   to shelter and to protect me.

America, with her plentiful land,
   will now always be my home.
And no more through waves and foam,
   need my family endlessly roam.

A poem from the view of an immigrant
entering our country for the first time
through New York Harbor.

Becky Willkens
Age: 13

The sailors are out to sea because the sea is very still.
I wish I could go out with them and I will.
With my imagination I can go anywhere.
I even can go inside the cave of a big black bear.
I will go out to sea and watch the dolphins play.
I'll go out to sea on this beautiful morning day.
And when I'm on the peaceful sea
No monster will come near.
Because they know that
I, the captain of the sea, is here.

Kimm Lincoln
Age: 9

E rin Gardner is my sister,
R ight now she's at school.
I think she's smart!
N ow, do you think she's the best?

Lauren Gardner
Age: 8

HALLOWEEN

Ghosts 'n goblins 'n costumes 'n candy
I think Halloween is just dandy,
But, here's some advice to go with the sweets.
The trick is - don't eat too many treats.

Tiffany Barnes
Age: 10

fruit
juicy tasty
refreshing sharing flavoring
apples oranges carrots celery
chewing gardening filling
crunchy eat
vegetable

Chris Veon
Age: 10

Leaves are on the ground
Leaves-yellow, red, brown, orange
Beautiful nature!

Jeremy Inman
Age: 9

Doughnut
round, chewing
tasting, refreshing, baking
icing, cake, cashew, walnut
wrapping, trying, eating
good, small
Nut

Kyria Shipp
Age: 10

Dinosaurs
huge elderly
fighting running climbing
bones fossils fins skins
swimming hunting eating
long harmful
Whales

Greg Schmidt
Age: 10

SENRYU

My cat and I play,
We cuddle up and sleep good,
The next day we walk.

Amanda Prothero
Age: 8

softball
fast, athletic
hitting, catching, running
glove, bat, catcher, umpire
boring, playing, sitting
fun, wonderful
baseball

Lauren Pierce
Age: 10

carrot
orange, tall
swallowing, slicing, eating
food, top, Popeye, fringe
chewing, growing, tasting
yucky, vegetable
spinach

Ardell Montgomery
Age: 10

WHALES

Whales live in the ocean with other fish.
Swish, swish, swish.
When whales gets hungry
they swim down deep
and up they come
with a mouthful of fish.
Swish, swish, swish.
Here comes a school of fish.
For whales it is breakfast, lunch, and dinner.
Swish, swish, swish.

Jessica Brown
Age: 10

ON THANKSGIVING DAY

People gather round to eat turkey and corn.
Guess when that was?
It's when Thanksgiving Day was born.
Family and friends sit at the table.
While dad sits and watches the football games on cable.
After dad gets tired of watching the game.
He starts carving the turkey with the knife.
Then we pray for all we have in this special life.

Ashley Hileman
Age: 8

DARE TO DISCOVER

Dare to discover the path up ahead
Dare to discover the world around us

The oceans have a big tide
The mountains are very wide
The desert is hot and dry
Blue is the color of the sky

Don't cut down our flowers and trees
There will be no pollen for the bees
The sun comes up when we have fun
The moon is out when the day is done

Dare to discover the path up ahead
Dare to discover the world around us.

Crista Hill
Age: 9

Imagine a place way up in the sky.
A place where stars twinkle and unicorns fly.
A place where dreams happen,
And wishes come true,
A place for everyone,
Just like you!

Brittany Debo
Age: 9

LIFE

LIfe wiggles, and jiggles, and moves
   all around.
It does somersaults, and cartwheels,
   and hangs upside down.
From inside it glows outward.
From outside it seeps in.
   To fill, and bubble, and flow
     from within.
It gushes, and shines, and radiates
   from my seams.
From the day I was born,
   till the end of my dreams.
Life is a glorious God-given gift,
   it hovers around like a
     pearl-white mist.
Life extends to all nations,
   and will continue to burn bright.
   And will fade with creation
   far out of sight.

Kensy Chew
Age: 13

THE WINNER

The game is tied with ten seconds to go,
Tthe outcome of the game is not yet known.

A nervous coach yells, SHOOT, from the bench,
He points down court, then his fists start to clench.

She stands all alone as the ball reaches her hands,
And begins to get nervous, glancing into the stands.

She squares up to shoot and releases the ball,
She watches it arch and she watches it fall.

The buzzer goes off as it banks on the rim,
The crowd is hushed till the ball drops in.

The look of anxiety is gone from her face,
When she realizes her team has just won first place.

Tina Frollo
Age: 14

DANCING

Gracefully jumping up and down,
Trying so hard to get off the ground.

Leaping around from place to place,
With a happy expression on my face.

I prefer the music of modern jazz;
It must be loud with lots of pizzazz.

It doesn't matter if anybody's watching;
I am happy to be prancing to
     my
     modern
     dancing.

Melissa L. Kohl
Age: 13

lemons
sour, yellow
squirting, drinking, obtaining
tree, pulp, smaller, rind
seeding, skinny, treating
fruit, sweet
limes

Jennifer Consolo
Age: 10

73

leaves, leaves everywhere,
leaves, leaves in
the air,
leaves, leaves no more,
JUST SNOW AT YOUR
DOOR!!!!!

Kelly Cavanaugh
Age: 12

A DAY AT THE BEACH

Warm and sultry with miles of land,
Big blue waves crash into the sand.

Everyone laughing, playing, having fun
All under the bright rays of the sun.

Light colored seashells wash into shore,
Crabs and fish scamper on the ocean floor.

Children building sand castles tall and wide
Hoping they aren't washed away by the tide.

People wading in the cool ocean water
Glad that the day isn't getting hotter.

When the day is over and done,
They know that tomorrow will bring more fun.

Carrie E. Jacobus
Age: 14

Spinning and spinning, around and around
A brownish ball is thrown all around,
Up in the sky is where it belongs,
Hoping to be caught and not fumbled all around.

Andrew L. Guzzo
Age: 12

THE TROUBLEMAKER

Troublemaker, troublemaker, there you go again
You've emptied all the ink out of the teacher's pen.

You put a thumbtack on the principal's chair,
You stuck bubble gum in Bobby Joe's hair.

Troublemaker, troublemaker, you let the air
Out of the bus tires,
Thank God, so far, you haven't started any fires.

This time you've definitely gone too far,
You should not have spray painted
The gym teacher's car.

Troublemaker, troublemaker,
A war's going to be fought.
It will be on the day when you finally get caught.

Nicole Bush
Age: 13

Sunlight
Shines through windows
Everytime I look out
It shines so bright all through the night
Real bright

Amanda Garner
Age: 13

A STREAM

A little puddle
Grows until it turns into,
A long quiet stream.

Taryn Gray
Age: 12

THE YELLOW STONE HOUSE

There once was a cat that lived in a hat
and with that cat was a bug
that lived under a rug,
and with that bug was a flea
that couldn't catch me.
There was also a grouse
that lived in Yellow Stone House.

Cheyenne Marie Johnson
Age: 9

76

He goes on Saturday to worship,
And sits among his boys,
He hears the priest pray and preach,
He hears his daughter's voice,
Singing in the church choir;
And makes his heart rejoice.

It sounds to him like his mother's voice,
Singing in paradise;
He needs to think of her once more
How she lies in the grave
And with his hard rough hands he wipes
A tear out of his eye.

Roaming-rejoicing-sorrowing,
Going on through with his life
Each morning something new begins
Each evening watching it close,
Something attempted, something done
He has earned a night's rest.

Thanks, thanks to thee my worthy friend
For the lesson has been taught,
The flaming life has been forgot.
Our fortunes must wrought
It's sounding of an evil shape,
Each burning deed and thought.

Jessica Casper
Age: 13

There once was a man from Rome.
That got kicked out of his home.
He paid a dime to work as a mime.
But now he's living alone.

Mark Hunter
Age: 13

BASEBALL

The swing of the bat
The whiz of the pitch
The sound of the crowd
All going wild
The home run hit and
The sound of the mitt
As we won the game
In Notre Dame

William Walker
Age: 13

Jumping on my bed,
Falling down to rest my head,
Falling fast asleep

Amanda Dunsworth
Age: 12

Shadows
Jump out at me
Like eyes watching me
They look like monsters; bright shiny
Ugly eyes of terror.

Janel Gregory
Age: 12

There was a man named Paul,
Who went to the masquerade ball,
He decided to risk it,
And go as a biscuit,
But the dog ate him up in the hall.

Kasey Swanger
Age: 12

HATE

What is hate
are you just depressed,
or just a fate
lashing out or feelings letting go.

Jordan Greenlee
Age: 13

THE DOGS WHO HAD NO TAILS

All of his dogs had no real tail,
Until they sent one in the mail.
The dogs looked so weird,
And they had a beard,
And the dogs got sent to the jail.

T. J. Planavsky
Age: 12

SNOW

Is as white as a cloud,
Like a blanket covering the earth,
With soft white flakes,
Covering branches of trees,
With a shine.

Jill Davis
Age: 12

WINTER

Snowflakes dropping down,
Coming together like one,
It is winter time.

Mark S. Santucci, Jr.
Age: 13

DRUG FREE

Drug free,
I am drug free,
I am drug free for me,
That is the way we all should be,
Drug free.

Mark Allen Farneth, Jr.
Age: 12

CHANGES

As I walk through the leaves,
I can hear them crunch.
They fall from the trees like
Feathers falling from the sky.
Colors change like the rainbow fading away.
Fall leaves, winter snow.
Cold has turned even colder.
Snow is falling, flowers are blooming.
Spring is here and summer is growing.
You can smell the fresh cut grass,
Along with the beautiful smell of roses.
Summer is here, birds are singing
Rivers are flowing.
Time for another year of changes.

Jessica Horneman
Age: 13

The big sky is full of light,
As the leaves fall to the ground,
And covers up all the grass,
It makes a very nice sight.

As the ground gets covered mile by mile,
It's the sign of fall and soon winter,
All the kids go out to play,
So they can make a big leaf pile.

William Kersey
Age: 12

Hockey
Fast, dangerous
Fighting, scoring, checking,
Chelios, Hull, Richter, Potvin
Scoring, diving, gloving
Gliding, decking
Score.

Eric Mangone, Jr.
Age: 14

Jim's a ref at Polkland High.
He always eats a burger at half time.
He lives in Boston, Mass.,
So he comes a long way with a
Full tank of gas;
He also teaches a group of teens
Math in the gym,
Now they all say to him,
Boy I like you Jim.

Kristin Yednak

THE BIRD'S SONG

The birds are calling,
Singing a gentle fall song,
Softly calling night.

Jackie Lockhart
Age: 12

Come here now!
My mother said.
I have landed on my head.
Cause I was flying like a cow!

The kitten ate,
I sat here late,
I listened and tried
And then I felt like I had died!

I started to float,
Felt like a boat,
I called you,
And whew!

I came down with a splat!
On my bed I lay right now,
And tell you this story, OW!
I thought I'd landed on the cat!

Desiree Lanton
Age: 12

THE SNOW

The snow falls
like Niagara falls
it falls down
with a bad frown.

The wind blows the snow
and when it flows
it goes up
and down and up.

Jessica L. Rayburg
Age: 12

THE SUN

The sun is setting,
The sky is turning colors,
The moon will soon rise.

Kurt Sgalio
Age: 13

L ittle reptiles
I guana
Z ig zag guy
A lligators
R ealistic
D ots
S illy little creatures

Jon Sciaretta
Age: 8

THE SUN

The sun,
How wonderful,
Something glowing on me.
The rays of the sun beating down,
The warmth.

Erica Adams
Age: 12

MISS CATANESE

Miss Catanese, Miss Catanese
you are my favorite one.

Miss Catanese, Miss Catanese
you make learning fun.

Miss Catanese, Miss Catanese
you are   bright and cheery.

Miss Catanese, Miss Catanese
you made second grade never dreary.

Miss Catanese, Miss Catanese
you are the best.

Miss Catanese, Miss Catanese
you taught me to take tests without fear.

Miss Catanese, Miss Catanese
thanks, thanks to You.

Edward Adams
Age: 9

Spring
Green, colorful
Playing, swinging, jumping, cheering
Leaves are just blooming
Sweating, swimming, biking, skating
Scorchy, sweaty
Summer

Jessica Boyd
Age: 8

Where is it?
I've looked everywhere.
It's still missing.
I must fing it.

I looked under the seat cushions.
I looked under the couch.
I looked on top of the TV.

I can't survive without it.
It's not on the coffee table.
Nor is it on the bookshelf.
Someone help me, please!

Wait. What's that?
Over there under that chair.
Thank God, I've found it
The remote control.

Sean Blue
Age: 15

Summer
Green, sunny
Swimming, playing, jumping, visiting
There are green leaves not buds.
Chilling, falling, swaying, dancing
Cool, colorful
Fall

Holly Vivio
Age: 9

Summer
hot, colorful
jumping, running, dancing
Summer is pretty.
falling, prancing, walking
rainy, gloomy
fall

Karly Revetta
Age: 8

ONE GHOSTLY POEM

When ghosts come out on Halloween night,
They cause your body to tremble with fright.
Oh, how they scare you up and down,
Until you faint and fall to the ground.

Gregory Zenyuh, Jr
Age: 8

Winter
Cold, Pretty
Falling, Sledding, Chilling, Skiing
Winter is my favorite season of all.
Biking, Playing, Catching, Discovering
Warm, Rainy
Spring

Erica Butler
Age: 8

CHRIPY

I love my little parakeet.
He is so very, very sweet.
And when we play,
I have to say
He is so very neat.

He loves to sing,
While his bells ring.
Just a little green bird,
Who wants to be heard.

I wonder how it would be,
If he lived in a tree.
I wonder if he loves me.

Brandon Shutty
Age: 9

NATURE

The bluebird flew high in a tree.
   And at the flower was the buzzing bee.
The leaves began to fall.
   While the spider started to crawl.
A cow stood in the tall grass.
   And listening to them all was the
Fourth grade class.

Nicholas Doblick
Age: 10

THE BEACH

I hear the waves clashing, clashing,
  And children playing on the shore.
I go outside and see footprints in the sand
  And follow where they go.
They lead me to a special place.
  A place I can't describe.
A place made out of seashells with mermaids
inside.
The mermaids are so beautiful, with long
blonde hair,
And fins so green, they're as green deep, deep
Sea green!

Kendra Adair
Age: 9

SPRING

In the spring
the birds will sing.
The deer will run
and all have fun.

The plants will grow.
The rain will fall.
The wind will blow,
and streams will flow.

Jessica Orczyk
Age: 12

A SOCCER LIMERICK

I am a boy who's eight.
I like to play with Kate.
Instead of going to the mall,
We kick around a soccer ball,
Until the day is late.

My mom will open up the door,
And shout, Soccer will be no more!
She tells us both to come inside,
But if by chance the score is tied,
We stay outside until we score one more.

Alex Merlino
Age: 8

GAZING

As I gaze out the window,
I see trees and the sky,
1, 2, 3 counting the leaves.
Then I look at the sky and see,
Little white clouds floating in the air,
4,5,6 still counting.
Then as I gaze back into the room,
I see a teacher,
Schools in session!

Jaimie Valasek
Age: 14

TESTS

Tests, tests I hate them they're a pain.
After I study I never gain.
Math, reading, science, I hate it too.

It just gets in the way of me and you!

Teachers, teachers always give tests.
No matter what your grade is they're still a pest.
So leave me alone tests are not the best.
Now if you'll excuse me I need some rest!

Shannon DeMino
Age: 10

THE ROAD

There is a road.
It leads you to
the safest place
in the world.
It is a road you
know so well,
because it is a
road that takes you
Home.

Jennifer Sopchack
Age: 13

FRIENDS FOREVER

Friends are always here
When you have a tear.
Everywhere I go friends are always near.
I will whisper in your ear
A little closer come my dear.
You are my friend till the end.
Friends come to cheer.
Let's get some root beer!
Friends are kind of queer.
But we are still friends till the end!

Emily Jelinek & Nicole Gould

KITTENS

Kittens are lovable,
kittens are cute,
you'll love them forever!
As long as you live.

Kittens are playful,
kittens love yarn,
they'll play with it forever!
As long as can be.

Mallory Cable
Age: 8

THE FIRST DAY OF SCHOOL

It was the end of summer and all through the schools
The teachers were telling those boring old rules
Children were running and being real bad
The teachers were getting just plain mad
Matilda was passing notes and Carrie was too
Jack stuck gum on Karen's shoe
Tied together were Suzi's pigtails
In Lori's desk were bunches of snails
A frog was put down Stephanie's shirt
At Julia's head Sam threw dirt
Everybody was real upset
The teachers and students had just met
It was the first day of school

Megan Montgomery
Age: 11

SCHOOL

I like my hobby it's really cool
My hobby is going to school!
School is fun,
Although the books weigh a ton.
I like school.
It will always be cool!

Nathaniel Gray
Age: 10

FRIENDS

There are lots of friends
But there is one special friend
The one you laugh and cry with
The one you know forever
The one who is always there for you
You know you can be normal with them
They know that they can be normal with you
The ones who don't embarrass you
If they do you don't care because they are your
friend
Some things change, some things don't
But you know they will always be your friend

Ashley Tessmer
Age: 10

FRIENDS

Friends are nice
Friends aren't mean
Friends don't lie
Friends don't tease
Friends laugh and play
Friends help
Friends sleep over
Friends go home

Jennifer Palanti
Age: 10

Freedom
gentle, tender
relaxing, playing, eating
money, house, cuts, pains
working, whipping, yelling
hard, painful
Slavery

David Crowley
Age: 9

DAYS

Jolly-days are
Fally-days
Fally-days are
Funny-days
They're all days
They're all ways
Movin' to get to you!
Funny-days are
Sunny-days
Sunny-days are
Windy-days
Windy-days are
Schooly-days
They're all days
They're all ways
Movin' to get to you!

Nicole Richey & Shannon Nardello
Age: 10

School
Smells like teachers.
Looks big.
Sounds like chalk on a chalkboard.
Tastes like school lunch.
Makes me feel safe.
I think it's a great opportunity to learn.

Lindsay Holly
Age: 9

Halloween
creepy, spooky
scaring, howling, creeping
vampire, ghost, Santa, Jesus
playing, snowing, eating
snowy, white
Christmas

Meghan Fall
Age: 10

Moms
Moms
Moms
Small Moms
Tall, talented Moms
Intelligent, smart, working Moms
Brown haired Moms
Black haired Moms
Lovely, kind Moms
Nice, beautiful, Italian Moms
French Moms, too
Medium-sized Moms
Colossal Moms
Don't forget active Moms
Last of all best of all I like creative
Moms

Richie Polley
Age: 10

THE RAINBOW

Its colors are nice and bright,
Through the shining light.
With pretty colors in the sky,
Where all the birds like to fly.
Way, way up high,
Though it's fading,
I keep waiting to watch it go.

Deborah Ann Young
Age: 10

S ome people
P lay many sports
O r just like
R unning for a sport
T he most popular
S port is soccer

William Leszczak
Age: 9

R achel is my name
A thletic
C ute
H ug a lot
E xcellent
L istens

S. hidemantle is my last name

Rachel Shidemantle
Age: 8

Hissing, gulping down
Mice that run across the land
While finding others
That could be appetizing
To a reptile this size

Jonathan Snyder
Age: 9

B   aseball is
A   s good as
S   occer
E   specially
B   ecause
A   ll baseball games have
L   ots of
L   arge bags of peanuts.

Joey Schmitt
Age: 9

THE COLORS OF AUTUMN

Scarlet apples hanging to a tree all brown and bare,
Honey-colored weeds bending in the wind,
Getting eaten by deer,
Cinnamon-colored leaves dropping to the ground,
Maize dandelions petals falling to the ground,
Jet black crows flying South for the winter to stay.
Frosty gray squirrels burying their food.

Nancy Duan
Age: 9

THANKSGIVING DAY IS HERE

Halloween is over,
Thanksgiving Day is here.
I can smell the turkey cooking.
I know it is very near!

Pumpkin pie is good for me,
With whipped cream, on the side,
The turkey smells fill the air,
I hope it doesn't run and hide!

Shane Auen
Age: 9

TREES

The brown trees stood tall.
They were very very high.
Did they reach the sky?

Josiah Johnson
Age: 9

FAMILY

They look like presents under a tree.
My house smells like potpourri.
Makes me want to find a new sister.
Sometimes I wish I was an only child.
I try to kick them out of my room.
I think my family is nice.

April Kaparakos
Age: 9

COLD NIGHT, WARM HEART

It's a cold night,
The wind howls,
The leaves are falling.

I am alone.
I need someone to be with.
Here she comes, approaching quietly.

I recognize her blond-brown hair,
I look into her soft green eyes,
How lovely she is!

She sits down softly and curls up her legs.
Slowly her head finds a place and rests
in my lap.
I can feel her body next to mine.

I know when she's happy,
I know when she's sad.
I can feel how content she is now.

I rub my hand up and down her back.
The only sound is her soft meow.
She's my cat.

Anthony Lanza

HALLOWEEN'S DEADLY DEVIL

We can feel a rumble coming from below.
Fire starts to spread out from the ground you know.
Out comes something ugly, mean and fierce too!
It is the deadly devil coming to get you!

Nicole Abrams
Age: 7

I REALLY HATE MY BICYCLE

I really hate my bicycle I rode into a stake.
When I tried to get back on it,
I fell into the lake.
And no matter how I tried
I couldn't run away and hide!

Craig Yannuzzi
Age: 9

THE WORLD

I hear the world's desire.
I feel my heart's content.
I love the things the world gives to me.

I love the world's wonderness.
I hear Mother Nature calling for me.
I hear the birds singing.

I feel the breeze through the trees.
I hear the squirrels munching.
I hear the world's desire.

Carrie Bess Wightnight

UNBURIED TREASURE

Caring is one of the world's greatest treasures.
It cannot be found
    buried beneath the earth,
Nor kept inside a locked chest.
Look instead within your soul -
    open your arms,
    your heart to another.
There you will find a treasure,
Greater than any other.

Brooke Bejster
Age: 14

107

WISHES

One wish could make you rich or poor
Which do you want
I would want to have a train but not in the rain
I would want a snail and maybe a nail
I would ask to have a dog or a frog
I might like a cat or maybe a new hat
I could have a cow or I could learn how to bow
I would learn how to dance and maybe prance
I would order thread and I would bake bread
But for now I will settle for a friend that cares

Brittany Kinneer
Age: 11

THE CORNFLAKE

One brisk morning when I was awake,
I was attacked by a mad Cornflake.
It danced and snarled around my head,
It knocked me straight out of my bed!
It bit me on the nose,
It started nibbling at my toes,
Then it chewed at my eyes,
It also chomped at my thighs.
Oh, what a terrible mistake!
To be frazzled by a mad Cornflake.

Amanda Chrisner
Age: 11

ALONE

One day when I awoke,
I noticed I was all alone.
Where did everyone go?
Did they go to France?
Maybe they are in Paris.
My family may be here or over there.
They can be anywhere!
Where are they?
I don't want to be all alone,
In this cruel world.
I'm all alone.

Kelly Mardis
Age: 11

FALL LEAVES

Colorful as can be
hanging from a tree.
It's neat to make a pile
and jump in for awhile.
Jumping can be fun
as long as there is sun.
But when the sun's no more,
we have to go indoors.

Tara Hoellerman
Age: 10

GHOST AND GOBLINS

There he was eating a piece of pumpkin pie
I thought for a moment that I was going to cry!
That old ghost was up to his old tricks.
With those skinny white bones that looked like sticks.
He looked down at me and said, trick-or-treat!

Stefanie Stolitca
Age: 10

SCHOOL

School is cool
So obey the rule
Don't be a fool
Stay in school

Randy Higgins
Age: 10

HALLOWEEN

Halloween is full of black, orange, and green.
Green is a pumpkin stem.
Black is a cat,
Orange is a pumpkin on the witch's hat.
Goblins, ghosts, and witches all rule this night.
They run from door to door.
Trick-or-treat.
Trick-or-treat.
All the witches and goblins say.
Bobbing for red juicy apples they get lollipops, too.
Cookies, candy and popcorn balls
You can't stop!
This night is tops!
Candles all flicker in jack-o'-lanterns as
Trick-or-treaters hurry by.
You can see bats fly in the moon light.
Vampires dressed in red and black capes.
Fake blood drips from their faces.
You hear kids shriek as brightly colored
Orange candy corn is thrown around.
Trick or treaters make sure brightly
Colored wrappers are clean.
Then they go home for the end of Halloween.

Kristin L. Werry
Age: 9

THE OCEAN

The ocean is a mystery to me.
The force in it is something not to doubt,
But yet it is as blue as blue can be.
The tide comes crashing in and it goes out.
Now listen closely, this is what I wish.
I write upon this paper what I want:
To be a part of it just like a fish.
I only want to swim and not to hunt.
I sit along the white and sandy beach,
Imagining the wonders down inside.
But when I put my arm down in to reach,
They all just want to swim away and hide.
The ocean brings a smile to every face.
It seems to me that it's a special place.

Jessie Smith
Age: 15

WOODS

I love when I am in the woods
I am so quiet!
The deer can't hear me!
I tip toe up to them
I get real close
And then I s a y, B O O !
And scare the deer!

Julie Todd
Age: 8

MY COLOR BLUE

My favorite color is the color blue.
Because Christopher Columbus sailed the ocean blue.
It would be so free; it would be so fun,
Just sailing around on that big blue sea.

It is the color of the sky at day.
It is a color I would hate to throw away.
It is the color most boys like too!
I hope you like that wonderful color,

That lovely color blue.

Christopher D. Marso
Age: 10

PENNSYLVANIA

Pennsylvania is my state
Wintertime is really great

The Ruffed Grouse is our bird
Hemlock is our tree
You should see it in the breeze

Mountain Laurel is our flower
State song we have none
But we still have lots of fun.

Nathan Price

BLACK

Black is a color,
Sometimes in the sky,
There is a blackbird
Getting ready to fly.

Black is a color,
Everyone loves,
Oh look,
There goes a black turtle dove,

Black is so dark,
It gives me a little fright,
I always see it,
Every night.

Black is dark,
As dark as spice,
I just wanted to tell you,
Black is very nice.

Tonya Kunkle
Age: 10

THANKSGIVING DAY

I woke up Thursday morning and there was no school.
I thought to myself, this is cool.

I looked out the window, and there was snow.
I decided to make a snowman with a huge bow.

I came down the hill,
Rolled fast on my sled.
I soon fell off,
And bumped my head.

I realized it was Thanksgiving Day.
My mom yelled out:
You have no time to play.

Stephanie Underwood
Age: 10

THE SCHEPIS CANDY STORE

My family has a candy store
I'm the luckiest kid in town!
It's the best candy for miles around
I'm the luckiest kid in town!
It's called Nibbles and Licks
And I love every pound!
I'm the luckiest kid in town!

Nicholas P. J. Schepis
Age: 8

THE SEA

This is a poem about the sea
The sweet smelling water gets closer to me
As the shells roll up from the saltwater sea
A wonderful feeling gets inside of me
The hot cream sand touches my toes
The saltwater scented air goes through my nose
I see some fish jump in the air
A little tickle goes through my hair
As I see some fish float on by
A sea gull is flying up in the sky
I dream of an island with a castle in the sea
And wish that the princess would now be me
I hear someone call but think I am dreaming
And then see someone pass by water skiing
Now there's no sound for all I can hear
And then a hermit crab gives me a peer
Again I hear my short little name
And makes my brain go insane
Then I notice that voice of my mom
And look up but see uncle Tom
I ran like a dash
But looked like a flash
I slipped on my seed
And fell on my knee
Uncle Tom said Are you OK
Then Come on let's play

Molly Kernick
Age: 9

FELINE FRIENDS

Abbey and Daisy
Are my two cats.
Abbey eats Iams and
Daisy eats rats.

Abbey is a tabby
Daisy's grey and white.
Both are soft and cuddly and
I love to hold them tight.

Each one loves attention
In their own special way.
And they make me very happy
Each and every day!

Kimberly N. Stevens
Age: 10

WHEN MORNING COMES

When morning comes,
I get up out of bed,
Eat my cereal,
Brush my teeth,
Like Mother said,
And always feed my spider, Ted.

Matthew Whittaker
Age: 13

NATURE

I love to see the leaves whirling round and round,
  As they fall from the trees and hit the ground.
The sound is so pretty and the leaves are too.
  But make sure an animal doesn't scare you!

Julie Kavel
Age: 9

BUSTER

Buster is my dog.
  He is as black as the night.
When he jumps off of our wall,
  He always has a very fun flight.
He is the funniest dog I have ever seen,
  When I bother him he never gets mean.
Once in a while we buy him a bone,
  And when he's finished chewing it,
It looks like a stone.
  Once, one day, he chewed on our couch.
My dad got so mad he whacked him on his snout.
  He ran under the bed and he wouldn't get out.
When Buster gets better we will all get together.
  To me he is number one because we have so much fun.
Buster is the best--forget the rest.

Joshua Fedorko
Age: 8

THE SEA

The sea seems to go on forever
And never seems to stop,
With all the fish and seaweed
That floats along on top.

I wonder what is out there
Under all that water and those waves,
Probably lots of sharks
And some underwater caves.

I wish I had a scuba suit
So I could go right down and see,
I'd get all that sunken treasure
And keep it all for me.

Oh, the sea it is so peaceful
How I love it so,
I wish I could tell you more about it,
But now I have to go.

Ryan Thomas Devlin
Age: 13

WHY

Why is the world in a horrible state?
Why is being hunted most animals' fate?
Why are rainforests depleting at a terrible rate?
Why??

Why are drugs almost a necessity to have,
If you want to be a cool teen?
Why do most kids want to take drugs,
If it'll make them sick - do you know what I mean?

Why do we persist to deforest
Whey we don't really need half of the wood?
Why don't we just recycle the trees,
When everybody really should?

Why do we hunt the endangered species
Who just want to live without a care?
Why does every hunter have to get
An elephant, an eagle, a polar bear?

Everybody should help to make
The world a better place.
Instead of being greedy,
They should give with a happy face.

But why do we just lay back and relax?
Why let these activities worsen?
Why do they say, It doesn't affect me,
When it influences every person?

But, until all of these problems are solved,
Until many bald eagles fly free in the sky,
Until drugs and crime are a problem no more,
We'll sit back and wonder, Why??

David Guthrie
Age: 12

A WINTER SONG

It is cold outside.
The wind is blowing softly.
Snowflakes are falling.
Can you hear the wind?
It is singing a beautiful song.
It is the song I have never heard before.

Stacie Brentzel
Age: 13

I like fall and fall likes me,
I'm as happy as can be
Because the leaves fall down from all of the trees
And I play outside with my friends you see.
I like fall and fall likes me.

Katie Sandala
Age: 7

FEARFUL PUMPKINS

Nine big pumpkins on a starry night.
A little black bat gave them a fright.

This night is so dark.
Replied a small one named Mark.

Peek-a-boo said a big old ghost
That scared the nine pumpkins under a post.

There is also a witch waiting outside
Should they go out, they couldn't decide.

When the witch soon came near
They really went and proved their fear.

Get lost now
Or I'll make you a cow.

I will put a spell on you
So go ahead and shoo!

Ronald Rukenbrod
Age: 10

NUCLEAR WEAPON

Nuclear weapons blow up human beings
U S fighter planes have lots
Most bombs are lethal
They leave very big black spots
Bombs can be big or small
Sadam Hussien likes them all
He blows up dogs and horses
All he cares about
Are his babyish forces

David MacMannis
Age: 9

LEAVES

When the summer is over,
And fall rolls around,
The leaves turn crimson colors
And fall to the ground.
They are a delight to others,
But to me I have found;
They are a lot of toil and trouble
To rake them in a mound.
Burning them makes a pile of rubble
So I spread them on the garden-ground.

Steven Lane
Age: 12

KILLINGER'S SUNDANCE

Killinger's Sundance
  Is a horse,
But he's called Dancer
  For short, of course.

Dancing, prancing,
  Oh, what a sight,
To see him canter
  In the morning light.

Strawberry brown with
  A white star,
He is a beautiful horse by far.

Perky, frisky, and bright,
  He prances without
Any fright.

Killinger's Sundance has
  to go,
For he does not
  like to put on a show.

Heather Svesnik

FLOWERS

Flowers are pretty
Flowers are blue
Some are roses
Sometimes you go huchew!
People smell roses with their noses
Listen to flowers sing
Violet, green or anything
What do they say
You can find out in a day
Spring brings happy things
Like flowers that stand for hours
As tall as towers
Flowers!
Flowers!

Nina Rose Hapchuk
Age: 11

THE OLD OAK TREE

There was an oak.
Beside the moat.
There was a leaf.
That fell off when the chief,
Cut down the tree because,
It was infested with bees.

Stephanie Hoogerhyde
Age: 10

WHAT IF...

What if all the grass was blue,
And fish walked and people flew.
What if Lincoln hadn't died,
What if the Wright Brothers hadn't flied.
These thoughts in my mind often wonder,
And as I set here and I ponder,
The only thing that comes to me,
Is the only logical explanation there can be,
Is that the stone road of life,
Is paved with what ifs.

Lauren Wagner
Age: 12

THE BEAUTIFUL WORLD

Out here the bird flies free.
    The animals are trusting and gentle
And seem to know who you are.
    And want to be your friend.
The water in the lake is so clean and fresh
    You can see the pebbles on the bottom.
Sparkling like diamonds when the sun sets.
    The horses are like magic spirits.
It must always be kept this way
    For everyone who loves the world.

Cara Cecchetti
Age: 8

THE BICYCLE RIDE

Peddle the bicycle
really fast down the hill
peddle it very slow up the hill.
Let the wind hit your face.
Stop atleast a few times
to see your parents,
visit them for a little bit.
Back on your bike
off you go on your bike.
Go and go
until you came to
your friend's house.
Stop and get them
then go and go again.

James Sadler

FLUFF

Fluff is my bunny.
He is very furry
And sometimes funny.
Fluff is gray and fluffy.
His nickname is Fluff.
I love Fluff very much.
So does Mom, Dad and Amy, too.

Sara Halvey
Age: 8

I am my Daddy's boy
Though that may sound coy.

No matter what he says
I act like him in many ways.

From my head to my toes
And all in between also goes.

My temper, my mouth, and my nose,
But most of all, when I doze.

I become more like him
Day after day, whether bright or dim.

I am so glad to be my Daddy's boy
And not some dumb old toy!

Evan Shawley
Age: 10

THE OLD OAK TREE

I climbed the old oak tree,
So my brother could see me,
Even though I could climb the oak tree,
Please agree to climb with me.

Erica Renae Barton
Age: 10

HALLOWEEN

Nights are cool
And there's a rule.
On Halloween night
Everyone is all affright.
Spooks are near
And we are here.
Are we ready to say
Trick-or-treat?
There's orange and black
And even a cat.
Are you ready to wear
A silly hat?
Then we're done
And here we come
To count our pieces
Of candy.

Michelle L. Eaglehouse
Age: 7

THE DAY THE LITTLE KITTENS WERE BORN!

I looked all around and I saw two little fur balls,
all snug and tight.
I was glad it was not a fright
but soon came dawn and then came night.
Then I found out the most beautiful sight.

Ruby J. Nemec

SO MANY PETS

We have so many pets.
What can we do?
They kick us out
And act like a zoo.

John Ross Kuhns III
Age: 8

MY DOG FLUFFY

I have a dog. His name is Fluffy.
  He is so puffy.
When it snows, he goes out and gets a frozen nose.
  When I want him to sit down,
He acts like a clown.
  That's my dog Fluffy!

Kristy Rees
Age: 8

THE STORYTELLER

The day the storyteller came,
The sun was shining brightly,
And the breeze was blowing lightly.

But no one had time to stop and listen,
No one even showed his face
At the storyteller's favorite place.

For they all had school and work,
Too busy and important were they
To hear what the storyteller had to say.

But the storyteller sat and waited
Till the lovely day grew old,
And the warm air grew cold.

Has no one time to come?
Thought the storyteller in gloom,
No one but the flowers all in bloom?

The storyteller was still there at dawn
And the people laughed and cried, He's crazy!
For the only ones who would listen
Were two roses and a daisy.

                                    Kathleen McMichael
                                         Age: 14

MONDAY

A colorless gray sky
Lingers overhead
On this yucky, rainy
Monday
In the middle of
Bleak November.
It looms above me
As I walk down
Marguerite Road
To my awaiting
Bus stop.
I am sheltered from
The chilling rain
By a navy blue
Umbrella,
Adorned with
Little dancing
Butterflies,
Fluttering on the nylon
With graceful, gray
Wings.
Their color matches
The dreariness of the day,
In which
The swirling absence
Of golden yellow sunbeams
Prevails over all.
The fierce wind
Tugs violently at
The butterflies,
Trying to rid me
Of my shelter,

And we each pull
Equally hard
In a stalemate
Tug-of-war.
At last the wind
Gives up,
But spews forth
A final, angry
Gust,
That sends my
Thick, black hair
Whipping around
My face.
As I look
Down the street,
Through my
Dark, stringy hair,
I sight a crayon-yellow bus
Approaching.
I fold up my
Umbrella,
And feel the rain
On my face,
Descending from the sky
In harsh, stinging
Drops.

Jean Huang
Age: 13

I HAVE A PLAN TONIGHT

I have a plan tonight
At break of daylight
I decided to sing soprano
While my sister played the piano.

Kathleen Ketter
Age: 10

TIGER

Tiger is a special cat you see,
   Because he always plays with my brother and me.
He is number one because he is so much fun
   And sometimes he acts like a man.
And the best thing--he's all white and tan.

Phillip Dedo
Age: 8

MY DOG BEN

We got Ben when I was two,
You should see all he could do.

He'd chew on me like a rubber doll,
Then he'd run and make me fall.

He thinks protecting me is a must,
Especially when I go on the bus.

Ben is a wise old dog,
He even knows how to kill groundhogs.

When it's time to get a bath you can bet,
Ben runs away 'cause he hates to be wet.

He has a dog friend named Hansel,
They make a date every day and never cancel.

The two of them have so much fun,
Running through the cornfields in the sun.

Ben means so much to me,
He has become part of the family.

I will always love Ben,
And he will always love me.

That is something I can count on, for eternity.

Megan Colbert
Age: 12

GERMAN FOOTPRINTS LEFT TO SEE

German footprints left to see,
Leave a message, a message for me.
A message for all humanity,
A message for all eternity.

Russian's stern face,
Leningrad's citizens worried paces,
Looking for bombing,
German soldier's calming faces.

Nadia is unaware,
German soldiers start to care,
Caring for her and I
Lord, I'm afraid to die!

The message I think is clear,
Listen for you shall hear,
There's courage and kindness left in me,
And in German's as far as I can see.

Jeff Smith
Age: 13

IN GOD'S EYES

Who am I in God's eyes?
A bird, a bee, a butterfly, or a tree.

Who am I in God's eyes?
A person of truth or a person of lies.

Who am I in God's eyes?
Am I the roaring sea?

Who am I in God's eyes?
I am just ME!

Melanie Kozar
Age: 13

DID WHAT?

Dad, Dad,
I washed the dog
And fed the hog
And dressed the cat
And cleaned the mat
And cleaned the turkey
And ate my dog's jerky
You did what?

Jennifer Leonard
Age: 7

I LOVE MY FAMILY

My family is nice
My last name is Reitz
My name is Bob
My uncle's name is Rob
Then there's aunt Loray
She's always willing to play
My mom is great
She's never late
I have a cool dad
He never gets mad
My brother is tall
He's taller than all
I have two dogs
They eat like hogs
My grandma lives in Plum
She likes to hum
I have a terrific Pap Pap
But he doesn't particularly like to rap
I have a cousin named Zach
He's a lot shorter than Shaq
I have an aunt Terri
Who is married
To my uncle Pat
Who isn't fat
I have an aunt Suzie
I wish she had jacuzzi
I have an uncle Pete
He is neat
Aunt Maureen is cool
She's not a fool
Uncle Todd
Has a hot rod

My Pappy
Is always happy
I wrote this poem because
I didn't want to pause
In telling you how much I love my family

Robert J. Reitz,III
Age: 10

Whatif the sky was not blue?
Whatif there was no dew?
Whatif there were no trees?
Whatif dogs did not have fleas?
Whatif the sun did not shine?
Whatif dogs did not whine?
Whatif there was no crime?
Whatif criminals did not do their time?

Steven Wilt
Age: 12

TOMMY GREENE

Little Tommy Greene,
Is very mean,
He throws rocks,
At a big ox.

James Duffy Rice
Age: 9

141

SPRING

April showers,
Bring May flowers.
That's what they say.
Beautiful skies,
And butterflies.
On a perfect day.

The time of the year,
When the water runs clear
And the afternoons are warm
The green leaves are bright.
The garden's a sight.
But will there be a storm?

Jessica Marsh
Age: 10

KITTENS PUPPIES

Kittens and puppies are neat
They have four feet
They are puffy
And they are fluffy
I made this rhyme
And I used my time
This is by Monica
Who doesn't like the harmonica

Monica Majewski
Age: 9

THE CHRISTMAS PROBLEM

I ran down the stairs and to my surprise
I saw a big fat guy with a twinkle in his eyes.
Oh, no, my chimney is too small.
I hope he doesn't fall.
Santa, I'll get you out,
Just suck in your stomach and fly right out.
Oh my gosh, it worked.
Santa said, Thank you, my dear.
You've been a good girl all year.
He flew away in a flash
And yelled, Merry Christmas,
I hope the spirit lasts.

Kate Krentz
Age: 11

AUTUMN YELLOW

When the bright sun is shining,
I think of yellow things.
Of big juicy lemons,
And butterflies with golden wings.
I think of nice chrysanthemums,
In the morning light.
Of yellow leaves and harvest moons.
They're such a gorgeous sight!

Kathy Kaufmann
Age: 9

143

FRIED BEANS

There once was a man
From southern land
Who ate fried beans
And never raised a hand.

He lived in the streets
His family poor,
They had no walls...
Not even a door.

But every hour
Of every day
He sat on the street
And ate way.

And when he was twenty
He still ate his beans,
He was as tall a a house
And it weren't from his genes.

He then became forty;
He was as tall as a tower,
The houses all cussed
'Cause he had more power.

He lived to be ninety
When God took his soul.
He was fifteen feet tall
And he had to be rolled.

The docs checked his body
And all they said,

Were, He stopped eating beans,
That's why he lay dead.

So eat your beans
If you want to be tall,
If you do not,
You won't grow at all.

Jason Florentin
Age: 12

MAGICAL THINGS

Mermaids, trolls, unicorns, and witches.
Knights, dragons, ghosts, and goblins.
Wizards, warlocks, and Pegasus
But don't worry, it's only your imagination.

Elaine Chen
Age: 11

Once was a girl named Mae
Who thought she could dance all day.
While doing the jig,
She tripped on a pig,
Now in bed she must lay!

Katie Frey
Age: 10

NIGHTTIME

It isn't always quiet when you're asleep,
The nighttime creatures come out and creep.
An owl swoops down to catch a mouse,
Some other creatures rush to their house.
The moon shines brightly up so high,
So do the stars that fill the sky.
The time is late,
All the animals wait
Until the sun shines so bright.
We wake up not knowing what happened that night.

Katelyn Schultz
Age: 9

JUST IMAGINE

Just imagine you could...
Rule the country, Rule the world,
Be the queen of France, The queen of Germany,
Just imagine you could have anything you ever wanted,
All the toys in the world, or your own restaurant
Where you could eat anything you want.
Just imagine it and it could
Come
True.

Maureen Copeland
Age: 12

JAMBOREE `93

Well, it all started in the summer of `93,
As troop 1329 attended the Boy Scout Jamboree.
The bus left at night, after we packed our stuff,
As long as we slept, we knew the night
Wouldn't be rough.
In the morning, without a flag-raising drill,
We found ourselves at an army base, Fort A.P. Hill.
At the Jamboree, there are many sights to see,
All my fellow scouts did agree.
At the archery range, the guys try and try,
At least to come close to the center on the bull's eye.
The rifle ranges are the same,
Only here it's a little easier to aim.
Lots of action takes place at the lake,
So you can bet there are many pictures to take.
Merit badge midway, pioneer trail,
So many courses in all,
Disability, awareness and rappelling,
I don't think I can cover them all.
We always have our lunch Philmont style,
For a guy can get hungry walking mile after mile.
It was certainly a great week at Fort A.P. Hill;
Now, it's finally time for the final drill.
The bus came to pick us up last.
We will not soon forget the Jamboree now past.

Dane Maurer
Age: 14

CAMPING IS

Camping is fun with friends
Water slides with twisty bends
Camping is long, fun walks
Parents have long, boring talks.

Camping is relaxing
Don't have to worry about tax collectors taxing
Camping is swimming pools
Place where you can act like fools

Camping is good thoughts in kids heads
So parents don't call the FEDS
Camping is neat stuff in camp stores
So your days aren't filled with bores

Camping is the greatest thing
It can make you laugh and sing.

Candace Jean French
Age: 11

LEARNING HOW TO SKATE

I hope you try with all your might,
So you won't have to be up half the night.
Just take a class on how to skate,
Or you'll regret that you were late.

Stacy Kistler
Age: 10

THE MONSTER AROUND THE CORNER

I went into my greenhouse and look at what I found,
There was a really weird thing
But it seemed to be so round.
I went closer and closer until I was halfway there,
I looked around the corner and saw a big green bear.
I went to go to feel it but it turned around,
It said right into my face,
Hi, my name is Jed and I am a clown.
I wondered why it seemed so weird
But I didn't dare to ask,
The thing just looked into my face
And then took off his fake mask.
I didn't know what it was at first
But then it came to me,
It was a purple monster that looked a lot like me.

Tommy Brittain
Age: 10

THE MYSTERY BOX

Open the box and what appears.
A little puppy with floppy ears.
So cute I couldn't believe it's mine.
I wish you could see it with big brown eyes.

Crystal Fello
Age: 11

SCOTTDALE, PA

In western PA a man left his mark
On a small , little town, its skies gloomy and dark.
   This town was the birthplace of Henry Clay Frick;
His work caused pollution, but made the town tick.
   This work was, of course, making coke out of coal;
A good business for such an industrious soul.
   As his bank account grew, so did the town,
And rich folks from Pittsburgh began to move down.
   But quick disappeared the blanketing haze,
And with it the wealth of the coal and coke days.
   So Scottdale was left with what everyone sees;
An old-fashioned town with some good memories.

Nathan Kukulski
Age: 12

TURKEYS

T   urkeys are extremely
U   naccountably poor animals. It is not
R   ight to
K   ill them and
E   at them and
Y   et people do this not only on Thanksgiving,
      but all year round.
      That is why I will ask those people to say
S   orry to the turkeys.

Ivy Wang
Age: 10

PUNKY

Punky is my friend.
To our love there will be no end.
He has lots of soft fur.
I love to hear him purr.
He comforts me when I'm sad.
He doesn't yell at me when
I do something bad.
He will never hate me
No matter what I do.
Punky, I love you!

Nicole Leonard
Age: 12

FRIENDS

Friends are fun,
Friends are nice,
Friends are fun to play with in the sun.
Friends are cool,
Friends are fantastic,
Friends are fun to swim with in the pool.
Friends are the best,
They never are a great, big pest.
I like friends!

Ami Labuda
Age: 11

MUSIC

Music is a sound
That rings in my ear,
Music is a sound
That I love to hear.

There are many kinds of music
As you will learn,
And each form of music
In time to its turn.

Classical music;
Is short, sweet melody,
While romantic music
Is a lovely harmony.

Rap is cool
Some people might say,
But others like the variety
Of today.

Now you've learned of kinds of music
That, through the years, have come around,
For there's nothing like the sound of music
That could ever be found.

Amy Morrison
Age: 11

SNOW

I would really like to know
   When it shall snow?
All of my sleds are lined up in a row,
   Waxed, refinished and ready to go.
We have lots of shovels
   And plenty of sleds;
My snow suit and boots
   Are right by my bed.
All of the winter birds are looking
   For a warm place,
As the winter wind blows in my face.
   Everything is ready
So all we need now is a snow that's heavy.

Allison Petonic
Age: 11

BUT WHY?

Up, up high in the sky a
shooting star getting ready to fly,

But why a shooting star
getting ready to fly in the midnight sky?

But Why?

MeLinda Sue White

MY UNCLE

My uncle drove in the daylight.
And will be arriving sometime tonight.
He will be bringing us a surprise.
But he always tells cute little white lies.

Daniel Walker
Age: 10

SCHOOL

School is so much fun to me.
I am as happy as can be.
Learning and playing with my friends.
I hate for the school days to end.
But then I go home as you can see
To be with my family.

Mikaela Sarnese
Age: 7

SEASONS

Spring is the time of year
When new birth appears
When flowers are blooming
And no one is glomy

Summer brings, hot, long days
With the sun's golden rays
School is out
And everyone's running about

Autumn's crisp and cool
And it's time to shut down the pool
Fall is really a scene
But all evergreens are still green

Winter is harsh and cruel
Bringing the snow and cold
Sled riding and snowmaking is fun
But not for adults who run, run, run

Candice Presto
Age: 12

THE EVIL INSIDE

If you want to scare yourself, just grab a horror book.
Turn to the first page and take a look.
What you see will be enough to make you scream,
For the eyes staring back have an evil gleam.
It is fear's face upon which you are staring.
There is a sinful smile that it is wearing.
You try to shut out that horrid face.
It is the image that you try to erase,
But it lingers in your mind,
For an indefinite amount of time.
Then you hear someone calling your name.
You have no resistance, what a shame.
It is the book that is calling to you
And you don't know what to do.
You have to read it, that you know,
Because of that phosphorescent glow.
With reluctance you take it in your hand,
Now reason and logic you have but a strand.
When that book gets a grip upon your brain,
You'll have to fight if you want to stay sane.
For the evil force that has you as its victim,
Will never give in
Until it knows for sure that it will win.
Remember this message before you open that
Book of thrills,
Especially if down your back it sends cold chills.

Rebecca Riggle
Age: 15

POETRY

Poetry is wonderful,
It is a beautiful thing,
Whether you read silently,
Or it's something you want to sing.

We always have written poetry,
We never will let go.
We always will read poetry,
Wherever we may go.

Whether it's on a billboard,
Or on a card, or on a sign,
Whether it says, Construction Ahead,
Or if it says, Be mine.

Poetry is a special thing,
It is what many people desire.
Whether it's about wind or rain,
Or even about fire.

Poetry is astounding,
Even if it doesn't rhyme.
People will read poetry
Until the end of time.

John Cochran

AUTUMN EVE

ndow,
range and green,
palate,

ss slowly gathers,
As treetops turn to ghosts,
Children tell their stories,
Who is scared the most.

The land is now invisible,
I'll lay to sleep quite soon,
And I am calm and steady,
Gazing at the moon.

Jacob Bacharach
Age: 13

MESSY ROOM

The sock is on the clock
The book shelf is up to stock
The cat is under the bed
The bed is not made
Good-bye I have to clean my room

Danny Pribisco
Age: 12

THE AUTUMN DANCER

She danced,
she twirled,
she flipped,
and she whirled.

She loved the
beautiful autumn world.

When her emotions changed
her colors would vibrantly change too.

When harsh winter comes she would
lie lifeless on her back in the white winter world.

Kristen Oleksik
Age: 11

THE RAIN

It drizzles, it falls
It pours down in sheets.
Sometimes it's ice
Sometimes it's snow
But, you really do not know.
But, if you want to know the weather
If you want to know when it's going to rain
Be a weather man for your gain.

Ashley Jones
Age: 11

TRUE FRIENDS

Through all the good and bad times
that we've shared.
In all the hatred deep inside we cared.

Staring at all of our priceless toys.
They remind me of all of our precious joys.

True friends stick together all their lives.
Through the hurting, pain, and strife.

And all of the love is to behold.
Sitting there tall, black, and bold.

Justin Karlock
Age: 10

STARS

Stars glisten in the sky,
Shining like a crystal glass.
They speak to me in mystery
My heart and thoughts race fast.
Their twinkling brightness is their smile.
Their laughter aims at me.
And when they're falling hits the sky,
I feel that I am Free.

Jason Polinsky
Age: 12

I love to sing, laugh, and play.
That is the most important thing of my day.
I love to jump, skip, and run.
That makes my day fun.

Molly Jo Mullaney

H	alloween is scary
A	bat came to my house
L	ovely princesses
L	ovely princes
O	n Halloween it is fun
W	e go Halloweening on a Sunday
E	verywhere you look you see scary things
E	very year you get at least ten pounds of candy
N	ow it is time to eat it up.

Brigid Janik
Age: 7

WHO AM I?

It is so dark
So dark in here
Where is this place?
That I sit in fear

I try to reach out
With all my might
But all I see is
A tiny drop of sunlight

Where did I come from?
Why am I here?
Is there anyone I can see?
Is there anyone near?

It is beginning to rain
So damp and cold
But I feel myself growing
Strong and bold

I can feel the water
Running through my veins
There is no more loneliness
There is no more pain

As I open up I see
The world in full view
Everything looks
Peculiar and new

I do not need to boggle

My mind for hours
I know now that
I am a flower

Kelly Schneider
Age: 13

MY PET WHISKERS

I love him,
Right now I'm holding him.
He's just sitting in my arms.
Sometimes he will sit in the
Corner of his cage and talk.
He jumps when he gets attention.
I think it's funny.
I think he's a good pet.

Elana M. DiPietro
Age: 8

Drawing is fun.
I do it at night.
When I'm done,
I turn off the light.

Chris Urosek

IT'S GOD'S LOVE THAT MATTERS

It is really truly the most important thing
that matters
it isn't that you get toys or money
God and you and me know that
it's God's love is more important.

Erica Takoch
Age: 8

THE ANIMALS

The song of the birds,
The song of the bees,
The squirrels & chipmunks up in the trees,
The deer eating & eating all the grass,
They all ask,
Why all the litter?

Miranda Dietrich

The polar bear is very rare
So save the polar bear
And he will grow more hair.
But if you don't he will no longer be there.
So let's save the life of all polar bears.

Jimmy Connell

SPRING

Spring has sprung on the tip of my tongue.
The young and the old have just
Broken out of the cold.
The tops of the trees are back
To their leaves.
The frogs and the dogs are back to play.
Well, hey, spring came in today.
See you, I'm going out to play.

Bobby Stillwagon
Age: 13

The skies were once bright
with the bald eagle in flight.
Like the wind he would soar,
and there were so many more.

Now the skies are all gray,
it's man's fault, they say.
The bald eagle is rare
and the nests, they are bare.

We should care for the few,
left behind in the dew.
For the bald eagle shows grace
to America, our place.

Bobby Topper

HOW DOES? WHY DOES?

How does a bird build its nest?
When does a tree look its best?
How does a bee make its honey?
Why are some days so very, very sunny?
I do not know the answers,
Maybe I never will.
All that I do know is that
I love them still.

Rachael Jo Knor
Age: 10

FALL

The air so cool
The leaves so crisp
Jack Frost is painting in our midst.

Summer is finished
School has begun
No more days to bathe in the sun.

Creatures are scurrying to and fro
Gathering food before the first snow.

One season's done
Another's begun
So get out your coat and go have some fun!

Ricki Geller
Age: 12

FLOWERS

Flowers are nice
But they don't like ice.
They are pink and white
Without any fright.
They bloom in spring
Hear the church bells ring.

Nicole Carolla
Age: 11

INFINITY

Sun impressing with fervid creativity,
Moon glowing in splendid vigor.
Stars smiling with leisure and delight,
Wind as swift as light.
Sky cloudy with pleasure,
Oceans full of observation and treasure,
Air omnipotent, powerful in great measure.
Celestial bodies waiting for discovery,
Our universe gives us exceptional vision
And insight.

Leah Walsh
Age: 11

SCRATCHING IN THE WALLS!

I hate mice when they squeak all night!
Will they climb up into my bed and bite?
First, they chewed a hole in the wall,
Then they chewed through the head of my doll!
I got mad, enough is enough!
So Dad went and got some of that D-Con stuff.
They ate one box and then another,
They took some back to their sister and mother.
Now everything is fine in my bedroom once more,
Dad's D-Con stuff sure was the cure!

Melissa Anne Landman
Age: 13

ME

As I sit under a willow tree,
  I think of all the things I could be.
Like a bird in spring that spreads its wings
  And flies down to a nearby tree.
Or a leaf that suddenly falls from its branch
  And lays on its back
And watches the sparrow pass.
  Or I could be a hotel tree
And have all my animal friends live in me.
  But when I stop to look around,
I do not see a bird,
  A leaf or a tree.
All I see is plain old me.

Emily Hogan
Age: 9

Fall is already here,
No need to wait any longer.
Winter is just around the corner,
The ground will be as white as a cloud.

Then comes spring and summer.
Also days are longer in the spring and summer,
And in the winter and fall days become shorter.

Jodi Burnsworth
Age: 10

IN GOD'S EYES

There's a sparkle in my God's eyes today.
  He said I put it there in my own way.
I said, How could I have, I'm just a kid.
  He smiled and said, You really did.
God sees only the good in me
  And forgives the bad.
And I try really hard not to make Him sad.
  God accepts me for who I am.
For He is the shepherd and I am His lamb.

Julie Hogan
Age: 12

ERASE

Erase the sun
To be undone.
Erase the moon
To come so soon.
Erase a star
To see so far.
Erase the world
Erase, erase.

Gina Buchheit
Age: 13

SIGNS OF WINTER

Signs of winter are
When Christmas comes around.
When children dance and frolic
In the snow upon the ground.
When snowmen smile their smiles so brown
And snow comes down, down, down.

Phillip D. Provance
Age: 10

TORNADO!

The clouds were dark across the world.
A twister came, it was just a big whirl.
The trees were bending back and forth
and one fell down towards the north.
The winds were strong
and the sounds were loud,
when the tornado left we all looked around.

Andrea Eppinger
Age: 10

THE UNICORN'S TRAIL

Listen to the hoofbeats ring,
As raindrops fall and bluebirds sing,
The trees and plants bend and sway,
The sunshine fades,
There is no more day.

The moon it rises,
Pale light it brings.
The animals gather,
The cricket sings.
The darkness gathers,
The shadows sway.
The unicorn comes to prance and play.

A little flicker,
A whited light.
It is coming,
To catch the night.

It steps inside,
The animals gathering.
It struts its pride,
Its beauty enchanting.

The unicorn stands,
It turns its head.'
It raises its horn,
A look of dread.

Then a light,
A magical kind,
Falls and grasps,

The withered night.
And all the animals look and listen,
As the full moon shines,
And the unicorn glistens.

And all the animals,
From far and wide,
Come one and all,
From the countryside,
To look and know,
To watch the unicorn,
And the moonlight show.

The light slowly fades,
It withers and sways,
The night is dark,
The animals play.
The unicorn is silent,
In the dark of night.
Then it runs off,
In a flash of light.

The animals follow,
The unicorn's trail.
Running by hollow woods,
And small flowing brooks,
Moonlit fields,
And darkened nooks.

The unicorn's world,
Is a magical place.
Where every dream,
One and all are true.
The grass is green,

The skies are blue.

So when the night,
Conquers the day,
And the unicorn returns,
To prance and play,
The trail to follow,
Is as plain as can be,
Although his world,
We can never see.

Courtney Adams
Age: 12

WHAT I WANT TO KNOW

How do bees make their honey?
  How do bees make their money?
Do robins chirp to be polite?
  Do black birds ever have a fight?
How does grass grow through
  The rain and wind and snow?
This is not all I want to know.
  But right now, I have to go.

Nora Jean Rekouche
Age: 10

THE WORLD

The world is hard to figure out.
When thinking of the earth...
Think of the stars as soldiers protecting all
below.
We turn and spin but do not know...
We're carrying out His loving plan.
If only we could see and trust His loving hand.

Laura Fleming
Age: 10

SCHOOL'S BACK

School is back,
Put your coat on the rack.

The teachers are nice the cooks are mean,
Don't eat their food it will turn you green.

Homework isn't fair but I don't care
But I still do my share.

Stacy Walker
Age: 11

A GLANCE BEHIND

I walk quietly
along the sandy beach,
mourning you,
lost at sea.

I hear a voice
and glance behind,
only to see dancing shadows
from the trees.
Could yours be hidden within?

I pull my dark cloak close
from the wind,
to provide the comfort
your warm arms
used to give.

I hear a whisper
and turn my head.
A leaf skitters
across the hard paved sidewalk.
My tears fall like rain-
steadily.
I realize you'll be here no more,
to share our cloudy dreams.

I quicken my pace
and head for home,
dreaming of your love,
hoping someday that I
might see you again.

I pass a sleeping stranger stretched
upon a stark wooden bench-
lonely silence fills the air.

Black waves roll in and out
not caring,
not feeling my sadness.
Just moving in and out,
unaware of my love-
lost at sea.

Kathryn Ober
Age: 13

WINTER

When the frost bites your toe,
When the wind starts to blow,
When the trees are bare,
When you layer what you wear,
When the snow is on the ground,
When the birds do not sound,
You will know it's winter.

Blythe Andrews
Age: 10

THE ENVIRONMENT...

The environment is dirty and we should clean it
up
I hate to look at land fills when the are all filled
up
We've got to get involved like Captain Planet
does
Reduce, reuse, recycle, it's good for all of
us.

Tyler LaCroix
Age: 11

WHY?

Why am I here on this earth?
Is it because of my human birth,
Or is it my Heavenly Father's wish?

I am here to tell people of the Lord,
That will pierce their hearts like a
two-edged sword.
This is my goal and my wish.

Matthew Mayer
Age: 17

HORSES

Horses are chestnut, silver, and gold
Horses can be courageous and bold.
Their musical rhythm is in their hooves
They clitter and clatter when they move.
Chestnut, silver, and gold,
You sometimes cry when they are sold
But they are always in your heart
Even when you are far apart.

Sarah Bird
Age: 11

Baseball is my favorite thing to do.
It might be yours too.
Once I took a chop at the ball
And I didn't think it would ever fall.

Tommy Guess

Last night I was playing house.
My dog Spot saw a mouse.
Once I thought I saw another.
Then I screamed for my mother.

Carly Ann Cole

I like football.
It's my favorite sport of all.
I play it in summer and
I play it in the fall.

Stephen Hohol

SCHOOL'S IN

When school is in
  Some kids smile
    And that makes teachers grin.

Lori Ann Patterson
Age: 10

MY DOG SPOT

I had a dog named Spot,
He ran around a lot.
Spot would sit in a pot,
Whenever he got hot.

Melissa Kuhn
Age: 8

B.J.
very good.
good in math,
he eats ice cream,
B.J.

Benjamin Sarnese
Age: 7

F amilies are fun
A nd we have it
M y family has a lot of love
I t is fun having two sisters and a brother
L oving my family is special to me
Y ou will always be in my love

Chelsie Detore
Age: 8

OCTOBER

Magic, magic in the air
Everywhere!
Beware of October
And magic!

Amanda Jayne Fox
Age: 8

BASEBALL

Baseball's really fun
I really like playing it
Pitching is the best

Brandon Woods
Age: 9

K   ind of movement
I   t can be fast or slow
C   ould be high or low
K   eeper protects the goal

Craig Slaubaugh
Age: 10

Moonlight shining down
creatures lurking and spying
darkness covering the sky
when the people are inside
with stars filling up the sky

Brandon Potter
Age: 9

Beautiful flowers
With smells of spring in the air
Butterflies flying
While sparkling snow melts quickly
With rosebuds starting to bloom.

Frank Gregg
Age: 9

T-Rex
Cool, Strong
Fast, Scrape, Bite
Mighty Animal
Giant Of The Earth

Nathan Jara
Age: 9

Love is like a bird,
ready to spread it's wing,
and to be heard.

Jessica McKay

Eyes look
Through the window
Like snow falling down
They welcome me;
Bright white flakes of snow.

Dana Swanger
Age: 13

As the snow falls down,
It covers the ground gently,
Snow is very cold.

Matthew Gaudy
Age: 14

Calling through the air
A robin's early spring chirp
Waking up nature.

Brian Krugle
Age: 12

NATURE

Nature is our life,
It's where living things come from,
It's our resting spot.

David McDonald
Age: 12

Sunflowers shine so bright
In the sunny daylight.
I water them day and night
Sunflowers shine so bright.

Gina Santucci
Age: 12